THE Crayola COUNTING BOOK

MARI SCHUH

LERNER PUBLICATIONS ◆ MINNEAPOLIS

TO THE MARTIN COUNTY LIBRARY

Official Licensed Product
Lerner Publications Company
A division of Lerner Publishing Group, Inc.
241 First Avenue North
Minneapolis, MN 55401 USA

For reading levels and more information, look up this title at www.lernerbooks.com.

Main body text set in Billy Infant Regular 24/30.
Typeface provided by SparkyType.

Library of Congress Cataloging-in-Publication Data

Names: Schuh, Mari C., 1975-
Title: The Crayola counting book / by Mari Schuh.
Description: Minneapolis : Lerner Publications, [2018] | Series: Crayola concepts | Audience: Age 4-9. | Audience: K to grade 3. | Includes bibliographical references and index.
Identifiers: LCCN 2016050901 (print) | LCCN 2016051876 (ebook) | ISBN 9781512432886 (lb : alk. paper) | ISBN 9781512455687 (pb : alk. paper) | ISBN 9781512449242 (eb pdf)
Subjects: LCSH: Counting—Juvenile literature. | Addition—Juvenile literature. | Subtraction—Juvenile literature. | Crayons—Juvenile literature.
Classification: LCC QA113 .S388819 2018 (print) | LCC QA113 (ebook) | DDC 513.2/11—dc23

LC record available at https://lccn.loc.gov/2016050901

Manufactured in the United States of America
1-41819-23779-3/7/2017

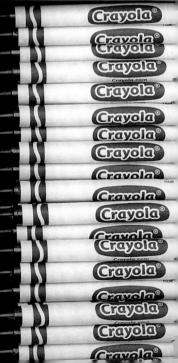

Table of Contents

COUNTING FUN

So many crayons! So many colors!
How many crayons do you see?

Let's count!

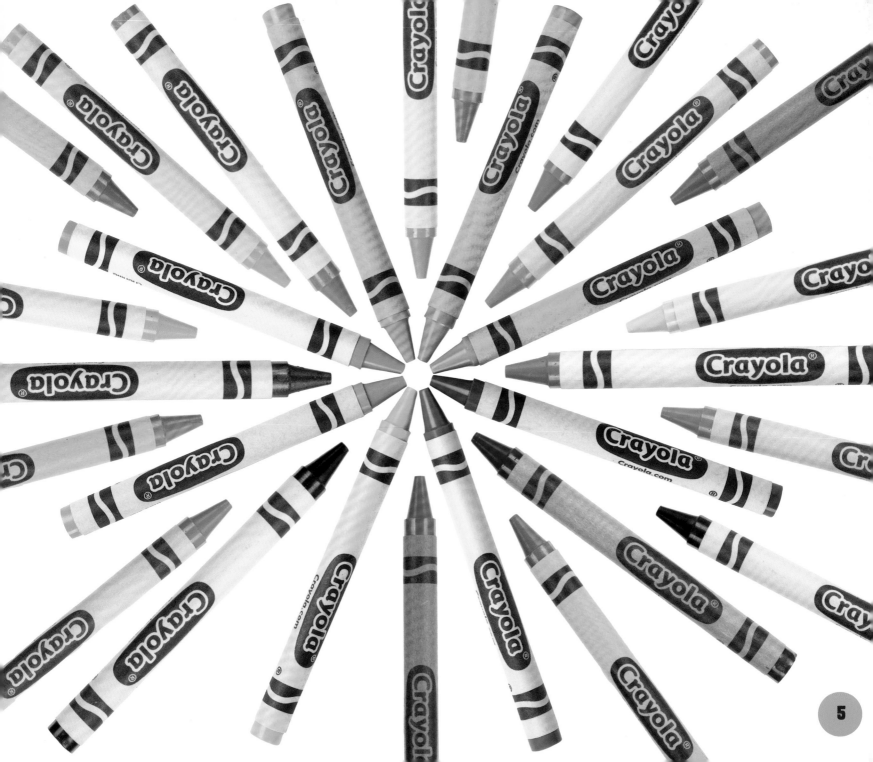

How many crayons are there? Let's count them one at a time.

Start with the red crayon.

1, 2, 3, 4, 5

Keep going!

6, 7, 8, 9, 10

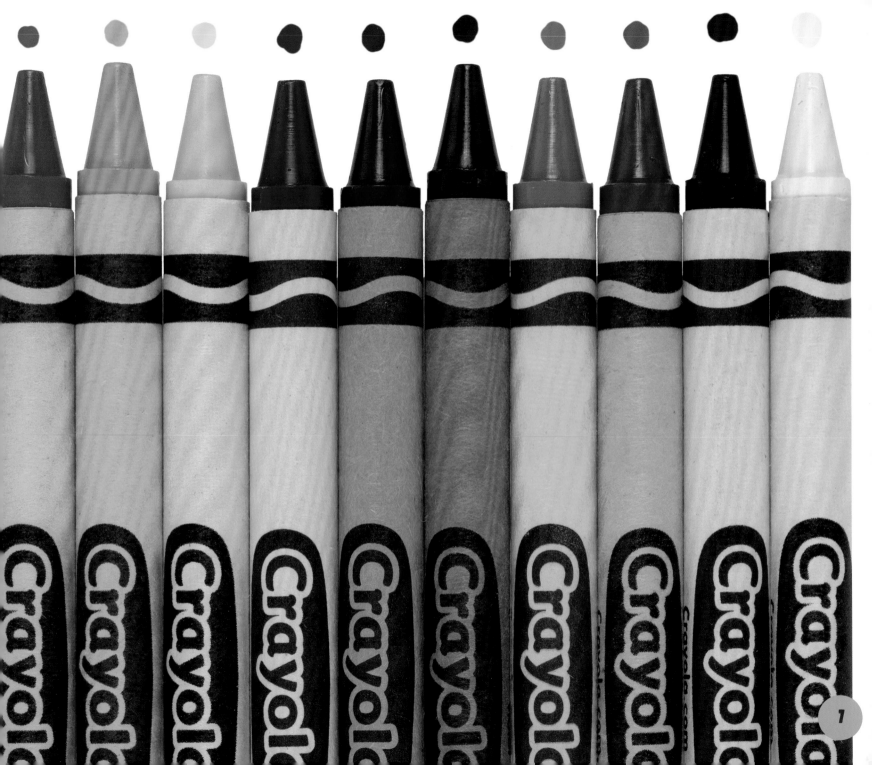

1

You can count backward too.

Start with the red crayon again.

10, 9, 8, 7, 6

You're almost done!

5, 4, 3, 2, 1

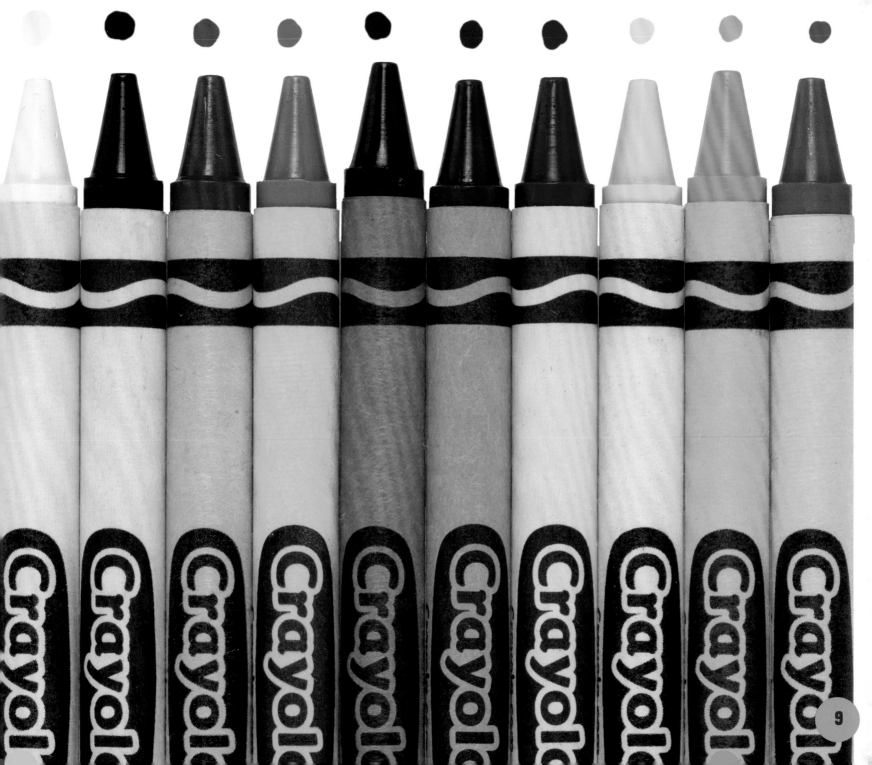

This time, count by color.

How many green crayons are there?

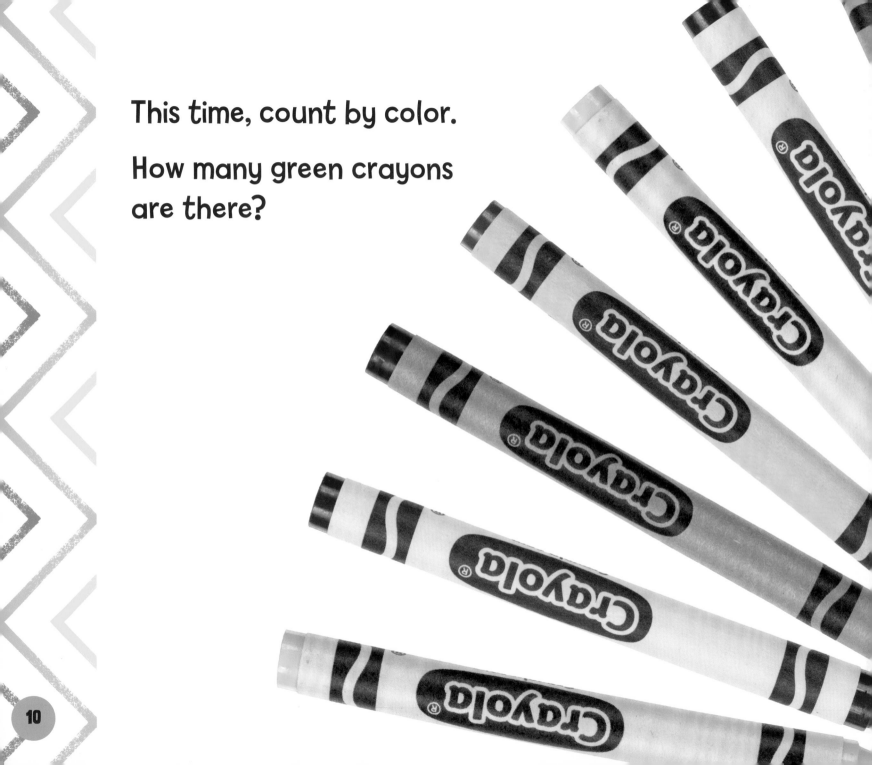

SKIP COUNTING

Let's count by groups. This is called skip counting. You can count by twos.

Look closely at the crayons. Each pair has **2** crayons.

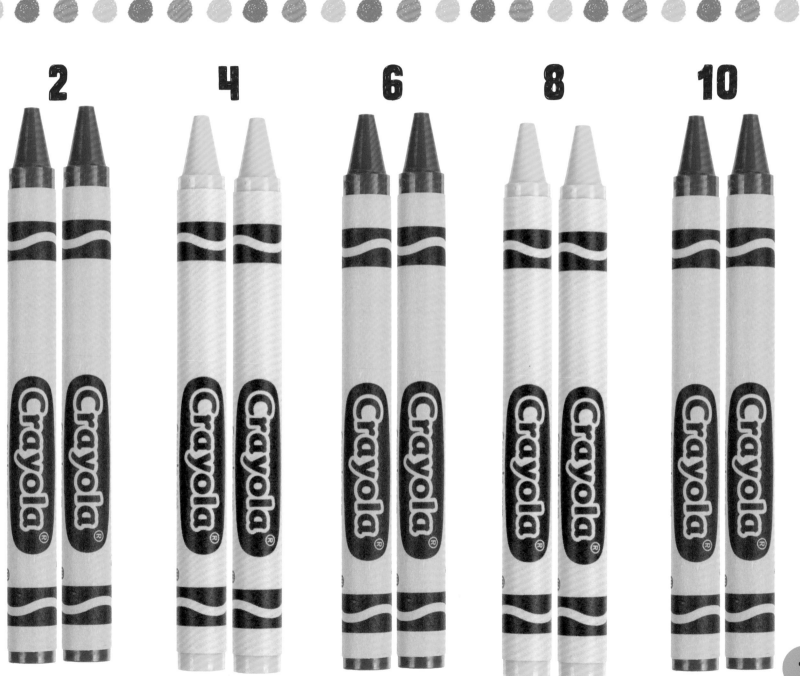

2   4   6   8   10

Now each group has **5** crayons.

5

10

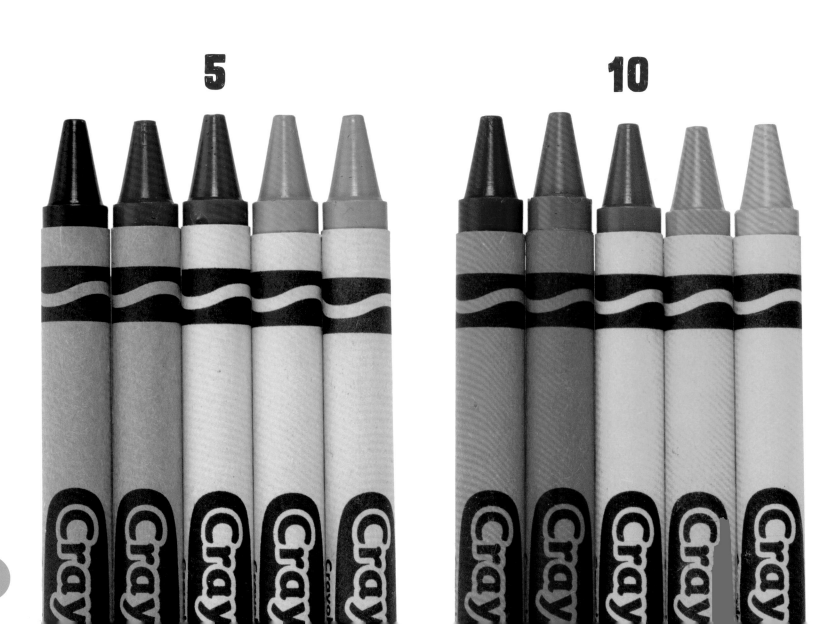

Let's count!

15

20

COUNT THEM ALL

Let's count by tens. Each group has **10** crayons.

Here we go!

10

20

30

40

50

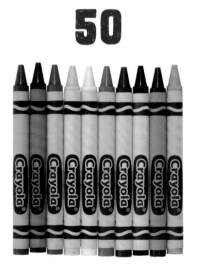

There are five more groups to count.

60

70

80

90

100

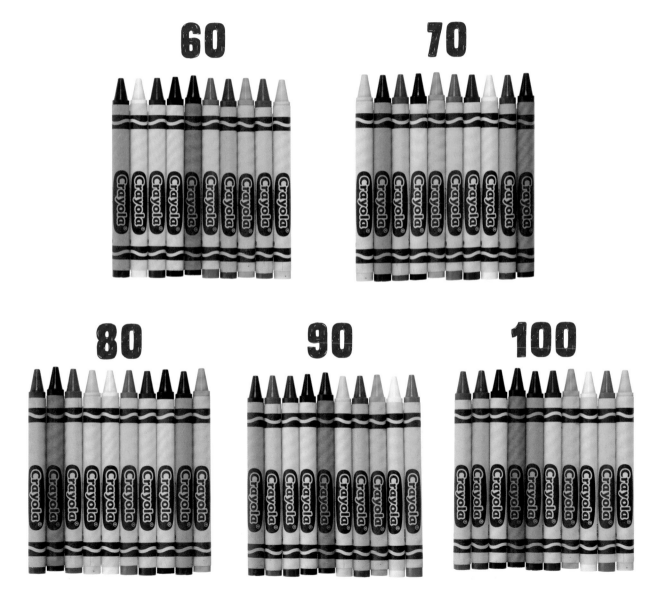

ADDING AND SUBTRACTING

Now it's time to add! There are **6** crayons in the box. There are **2** crayons on the table.

Add them together. How many crayons are there?

$$6 + 2 = 8$$

Now let's take **5** crayons out of the box.
How many crayons are left?

Let's subtract.

$$8 - 5 = 3$$

There are **3** crayons left in the box.

Look at all the crayons!
There are many ways to count them.

How can you count them all?

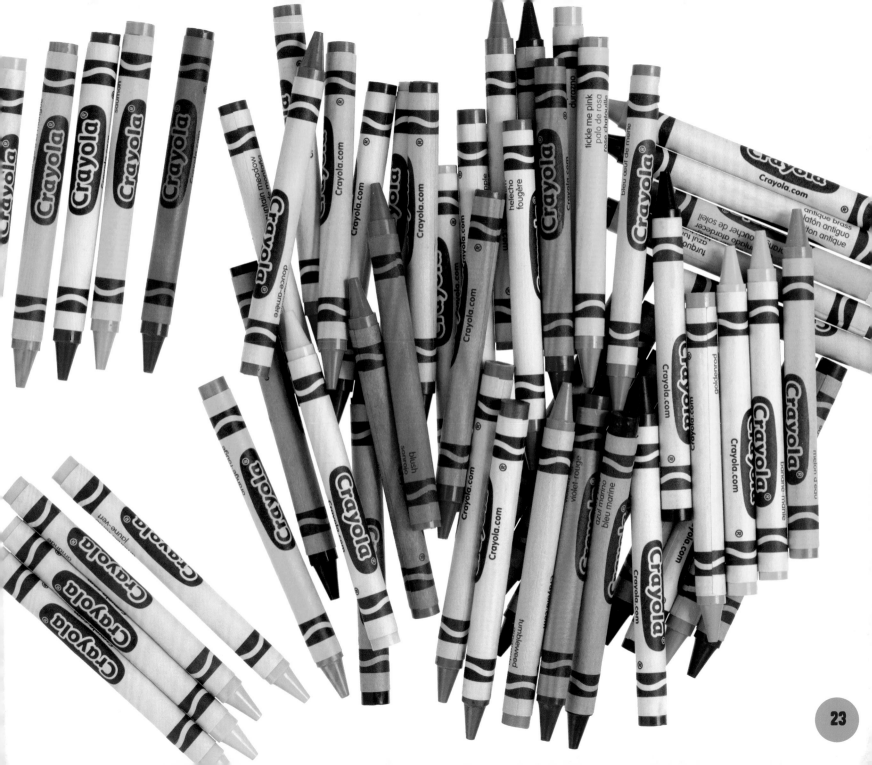

TO LEARN MORE

BOOKS

Brocket, Jane. *1 Cookie, 2 Chairs, 3 Pears: Numbers Everywhere*. Minneapolis: Millbrook Press, 2014. Numbers are all around. Count all sorts of objects as you read this fun book.

Higgins, Nadia. *Count It!* Minneapolis: Pogo, 2017. Read this book to learn about different ways to count everyday objects.

Rustad, Martha E. H. *On a Safari 5, 10, 15: A Counting by Fives Book*. Mankato, MN: Amicus, 2017. Learn about African animals while counting up to fifty by fives.

WEBSITES

Celebration Countdown Chain
http://www.crayola.com/crafts/celebration-countdown-chain-craft/
Practice counting with this countdown chain! You can count down the days until your birthday, a favorite holiday, or an exciting day coming up!

Skip Counting
http://www.abcya.com/number_bubble_skip_counting.htm
Check out this website to practice skip counting with different number groups.

INDEX

PHOTO ACKNOWLEDGMENTS

Images courtesy of Crayola and Independent Picture Service.

LERNER SOURCE

Expand learning beyond the printed book. Download free, complementary educational resources for this book from our website, www.lerneresource.com.